The trouble with
Tickle the Tiger

Words by Norman C. Habel
Pictures by Jim Roberts

Concordia Publishing House

A PURPLE PUZZLE TREE BOOK

COPYRIGHT © 1972 CONCORDIA PUBLISHING HOUSE, ST. LOUIS, MISSOURI
CONCORDIA PUBLISHING HOUSE LTD., LONDON, E. C. 1
MANUFACTURED IN THE UNITED STATES OF AMERICA
ISBN 0-570-06514-3

Old man Moses stood on a mountain
and looked across the river Jordan
at the lovely land of Canaan
with all its beautiful trees.

That land was the home
that God had promised His people
a long time ago.

As he looked at the land,
old Moses began to dream.
In that long lost dream
the land became the garden of God,
where all the animals live
in peace and love and laughter.

Right in the middle of the garden
was a tiny tiger called Tickle.
He was really only a baby tiger,
for God had made him last of all
and forgotten to give him a name.
The other animals called him Tickle,
because everywhere he went
he would poke his fuzzy whiskers,
his tailtip or toes,
into someone's ear
or under someone's nose.
And they would sneeze so loudly
that God would jump
and move some pieces
of the great big purple puzzle
He had mapped out on the sky.

God was so busy working
on His purple puzzle for people
that He didn't seem to have time
for tiger kittens like Tickle.
And somehow God had forgotten
to tell Tickle the Tiger
what kind of an animal he was.

And Tickle wanted to know.
Everyone else seemed to know.
So Tickle set off
with a big striped lollipop,
a huge bag of popcorn,
and a head full of questions.

Everywhere he went he tickled.
And when he tickled the animals,
they all sneezed and said:
"AAAAA AAAAA AAAAA CHOOOOOO!
What on earth did you do?"

Tiger, Tiger,
Tell us, do you fly?
Do you slink around the ground
Or soar about the sky?
Tickle! Tickle!
It's time this tickling stops.
You cannot go around the world
just licking lollipops.

First Tickle went to see
Happy the Hippopotamus and said:
"Would it cause too much fuss
if I learned to be a hippopotamus?"

"O.K." said Happy, with a wink.
"Jump into this mud
and roll around all day.
Make your feet all muddy
like children when they play.
Then later on this evening,
when God has done His work,
He'll have another hippopotamus
to give Him a good old laugh."

Well, as soon as Tickle felt the mud
dripping from his nose
like thick, black butter,
he gave a cough
and he gave a sneeze
and a very buttery splutter.
He sent blobs of mud
all over God's garden.

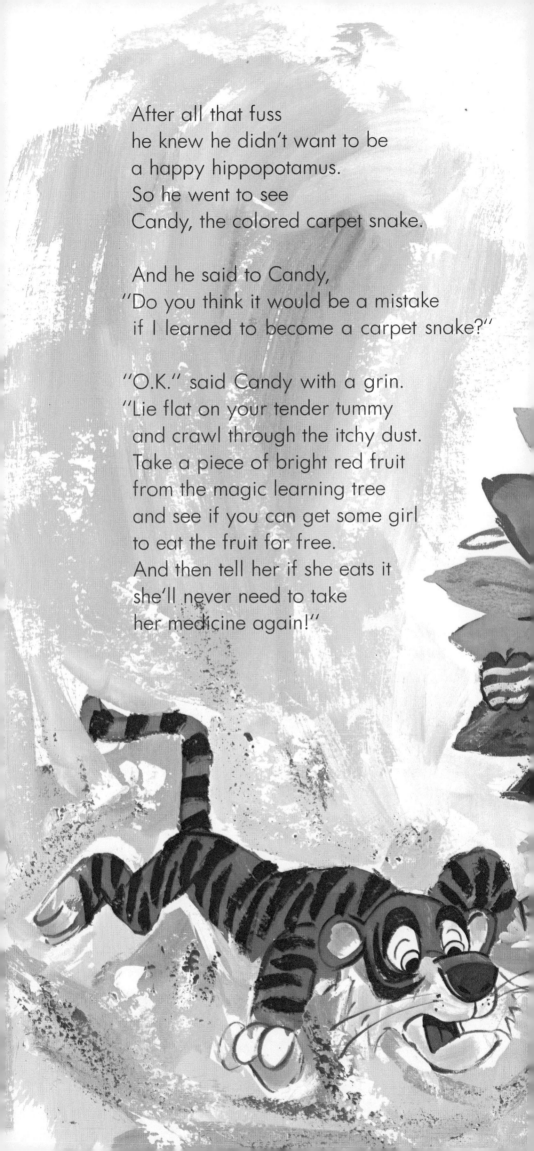

After all that fuss
he knew he didn't want to be
a happy hippopotamus.
So he went to see
Candy, the colored carpet snake.

And he said to Candy,
"Do you think it would be a mistake
if I learned to become a carpet snake?"

"O.K." said Candy with a grin.
"Lie flat on your tender tummy
and crawl through the itchy dust.
Take a piece of bright red fruit
from the magic learning tree
and see if you can get some girl
to eat the fruit for free.
And then tell her if she eats it
she'll never need to take
her medicine again!"

When Tickle slithered up
to this girl beneath the tree,
he had to scratch his itchy tummy;
and clouds of dust
swirled over all God's garden.
He looked so funny
scratching his itchy tummy
the girl just wandered off laughing
and licking Tickle's lollipop.

Everyone he met
knew his place in God's puzzle plan,
and when Tickle tried their work,
something always went wrong.

At last he went to see
Dingaling the Donkey, and said,
"Do you think I'd look like a monkey
if I tried to become a donkey?"

"O.K." said Dingaling, half asleep,
"Find someone who needs a ride,
like Abraham or Moses,
and let him dig his heels
into your fluffy side."

But everyone he met said,
"I'd rather ride a donkey
who was sleepy, sour, and bony
than ride upon a tiger,
even if he ate popcorn
with a face as sweet as honey."

Then all the kukaburras in the garden
started laughing very loudly:
"OO OO OO OO AH AH AH AH AHAAAAAAAH.
You look like a fluffy monkey
trying to be a donkey."

Well, that was it.
Tickle decided to go to God,
who was very busy working
on His purple puzzle plan for people.
In fact, He didn't see Tickle come up
and sit on a branch above God's head.

So Tickle took the tip of his tail
and tickled the tip of God's nose.
And God sneezed!
AA AAA AAACHOOOOOO!
How He sneezed!
He sneezed so hard
He sent pieces of the purple puzzle
flying all over heaven and earth.
And some of them are there still,
waiting for us to find them.

God looked at Tickle,
and He didn't seem very happy.
But Tickle said, "Good God,
would You like to have a ride?
I am learning to be a donkey."

God couldn't help but laugh
when He heard what Tickle asked.
"Why don't you take a trip," God said,
"and find the puzzle piece
that just now landed down in India?
And while you're there,
learn to be a tiger
with a roar that rules the jungle.
You'll never make a snake
and you'll never be a bee.
Just learn to be a tiger,
and that will make you part
of My purple puzzle tree!

"Meanwhile, I have a job to do.
That mighty sneeze reminded Me
that I must blow the waters apart
and make a path across the river Jordan
to bring My people home.
That's the next important part
in the purple puzzle plan."

Then, as all the animals said goodbye to Tickle,
they sang the purple puzzle song:

Tiger, Tiger, tell me, do you fly?
Do you slink around the ground
Or soar about the sky?
God made tigers! God made you and me
To fit together piece by piece
In His purple puzzle tree.

OTHER TITLES

the PURPLE PUZZLE TREE